# I SPY
# EVERYTHING!

WELCOME TO

# I SPY: EVERYTHING!

# GOOD LUCK!

# I SPY with my little eye, something beginning with...

A is for
ANCHOR!

B

is for

Book!

# I SPY with my little eye, something beginning with.

# I SPY with my little eye, something beginning with...

C is for CUP!

# I SPY with my little eye, something beginning with...

## D and E

**D** is for DEER!

**E** is for EGGS!

# I SPY with my little eye, something beginning with...

# F

is for

# Fox!

# I SPY with my little eye, something beginning with...

# F

is for

# Fox!

# I SPY with my little eye, something beginning with...

G

is for

GRAPES!

# I SPY with my little eye, something beginning with...

H and i

H is for HEDGEHOG!

i is for ICE CREAM!

# I SPY with my little eye, something beginning with...

J is for JACK IN THE BOX!

# I SPY with my little eye, something beginning with...

K and L

K is for KOALA BEAR!

L is for LAMP!

# I SPY with my little eye, something beginning with...

M and N

M is for MILK!

N is for NURSE!

# I SPY with my little eye, something beginning with...

O

is for

ORANGE!

# I SPY with my little eye, something beginning with...

## P and Q

P is for PIG!

Q is for QUEEN!

# I SPY with my little eye, something beginning with...

# R

is for

# RAINBOW!

# I SPY with my little eye, something beginning with...

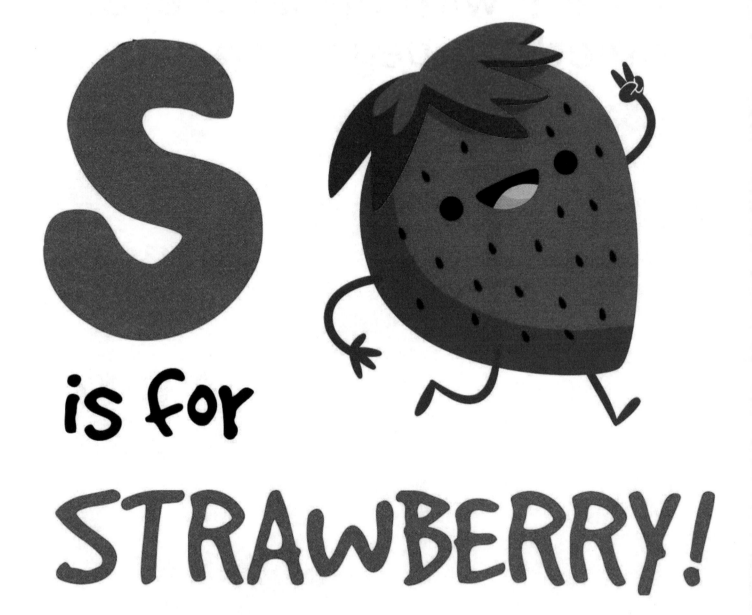

S
is for
STRAWBERRY!

# I SPY with my little eye, something beginning with...

T and U

**T** is for
## TABLE!

**U** is for
## UMBRELLA!

# I SPY with my little eye, something beginning with...

V

is for

VAMPIRE!

# I SPY with my little eye, something beginning with...

W is for
WHALE!

# I SPY with my little eye, something beginning with...

**X** is for
**XYLOPHONE!**

**Y** is for **YAK!**

**Z** is for
**ZIP!**

# THE END!

# Find us on **Amazon!**

Discover all of the titles available in the series; **including these below...**

I SPY
IN THE COUNTRYSIDE!

I SPY
ANIMALS!

I SPY
AT THE SEASIDE!

I SPY
CHARACTERS & TOYS!

I SPY
IN THE CITY!

I SPY
FROM A-Z!

You'll also love;

# I SPY – Color the A-Z!

Featuring puzzles for each letter of the alphabet, this book is also a coloring book!

## © 2019 Webber Books

Images and vectors by;

freepix, alekksall, art.shcherbyna, agnessz_arts, anggar3ind, Alliesinteractive, Anindyanfitri, Ajipebriana, Alliesinteractive, Balasoui, Bakar015, Bimbimkha, brgfx, cornecoba, creativepack, creativetoons, ddraw, dooder, drawnhy97, elsystudio, Emily_b, flaticon, freshgraphix, frimufilms, Garrykillian, gordoba, graphicrepublic, graphicmama, iconicbestiary, ibrandify, Jannoon028, johndory, Kamimiart, kat_branch, kbibibi, Kjpargeter, Kraphix, layerace, lesyaskripak, lexamer, lyolya_profitrolya, Macrovector, Makyzz, milano83, Miguel_ruiz, nenilkime, natalka_dmitrova, natkacheva, omegapics, Pickapic, rawpixel, Rayzong, renata.s, rezzaalam, rocketpixel, RosaPuchalt, Rwdd_studios, sketchepedia, stephanie2212, SilviaNatalia, Terdpongvector, titusurya, vectorpocket, Vectortwins, Vector4free, vectorportal, vectorpouch, vecteezy, VVstudio, Visnezh, zirconicusso